Severe Weather

Charmaine Robertson

Rosen REAL READERS

Rosen Classroom™
New York

Weather can be good.

It can also be bad.

Sometimes, weather is very bad.
It is called severe weather.

Thunderstorms are severe weather.

Tornadoes are severe weather.

Severe weather can bring lightning.

It can bring snow, too.

It can cause floods.

It can knock down trees.

Severe weather can be scary.

Good weather always returns, though.

Words to Know

flood

lightning

thunderstorm

tornado